THE NETHERLANDS

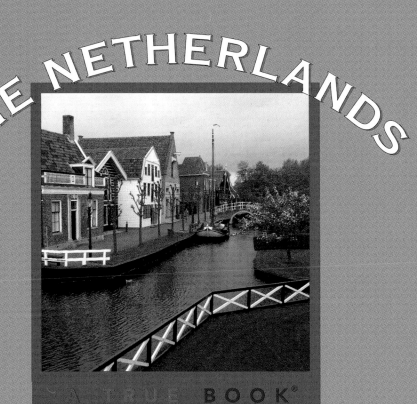

A TRUE BOOK®

by
Ann Heinrichs

Children's Press®
A Division of Scholastic Inc.

New York Toronto London Auckland Sydney
Mexico City New Delhi Hong Kong
Danbury, Connecticut

Content Consultant
Dr. Patricia Conroy
Department of
Scandinavian Studies
University of Washington
Seattle, WA

Reading Consultant
Nanci R. Vargus, Ed.D.
Assistant Professor
Literacy Education
University of Indianapolis
Indianapolis, IN

The photograph on the
cover shows a field of
tulips. The photograph on
the title page shows houses
along a canal.

A Dutch girl

Library of Congress Cataloging-in-Publication Data

Heinrichs, Ann
    The Netherlands / by Ann Heinrichs.
        p. cm. — (A true book)
    Summary: Discusses the geography, history, and culture of this small
country in northwestern Europe that is the world's largest producer of
tulips and exporter of cheese.
    Includes bibliographical references and index.
    ISBN 0-516-22675-4 (lib. bdg.)   0-516-27750-2 (pbk.)
        1. Netherlands—Juvenile literature. [1. The Netherlands.] I. Title.
II. Series.
DJ18 .H44 2002
949.2—dc21   2001008505

Contents

THE NETHERLANDS

Groningen

North
Sea

Haarlem
Amsterdam
The Hague

THE NETHERLANDS

Arnhem

Rotterdam

Rhine

Maas River

Rhine

N
W   E
S

BELGIUM

GERMANY

Meuse River

FRANCE

LUXEMBOURG

0   400 miles

0   600 kilometers

Living With the Sea

The Netherlands is a small country in northwestern Europe. Its people are called the Dutch. The Netherlands is sometimes called Holland. However, Holland is the proper name for only the western part of the country.

Germany is east of the Netherlands. To the south is

Belgium. On the north and west, the Netherlands faces the North Sea.

The Dutch people have always struggled with the sea. Much of their land was once covered by seawater. They built **dikes**, or high walls, to hold the water back. Then they drained the water into **canals**. These lands that were once underwater are called the *polders*. They cover almost half the country. The Netherlands's

Polders make up some of the country's richest farmland.

richest farmland and largest cities lie in the polders.

Many rivers flow through the Netherlands into the sea. The largest are the Rhine, the Maas (or Meuse), and the Scheldt.

The Rhine splits into several branches.

The Zuider Zee began where one branch of the Rhine flowed into the sea. Over time, it grew into a huge inland sea. In the 1930s, the Dutch built a long dike across its opening. Then they drained the water to create more farmland.

Land in the south and east is higher. People here do not have to worry about the sea

Bridges span many canals and rivers in the Netherlands.

flooding their land. It is made up of rolling plains, river valleys, and forests. Many bridges span the rivers, while dikes hold back their waters. Fruit trees grow along the riverbanks.

Vaalserberg, or Vaalser Hill, is the Netherlands's highest point. It stands in the country's southeast corner. The forested Veluwe region is in the east. People enjoy visiting its national parks and wildlife areas.

The Veluwe region is in the eastern part of the country.

Reclaiming the Land

For hundreds of years, Dutch people and their **ancestors** have been reclaiming land from the sea. That means removing seawater to create land for homes and farms. To do this, first they build a dike, or high wall, around a water-covered area. Then they pump the water out into long ditches called canals. In the 1200s, the Dutch began using windmills to power the water pumps. As the windmills' arms turned around, they moved the parts of the pumping machines. Today, most Dutch water pumps are run by electric engines. Water still seeps into the drained land. So, it must be pumped out on a regular basis.

The Dutch People

The Dutch people are tightly packed into their small country. More than 15 million people live there. The center section of the coast has the highest population. It is home to more than 6 million people. The major cities are in this region, too.

Many people live in the cities and they can become very crowded.

Amsterdam is the capital and largest city. Next in size is Rotterdam. This port handles more cargo than any other

The International Court of Justice is located in The Hague.

seaport in the world. The third-largest city is The Hague. It is the country's center of government. The International Court of Justice is also located in The Hague.

Most people in the Netherlands are Dutch. **Minority** groups include people from Indonesia, Suriname, Morocco, and Turkey. People from dozens of nations work in the big cities.

The Netherlands's official language is Dutch. Many Dutch

This jewelry shop sign is written in Dutch.

Many children in the Netherlands can speak more than one language.

people also speak English, French, or German. They welcome the chance to use their language skills with foreign visitors.

Two other native languages are spoken in the Netherlands. People in the northern **province** of Friesland speak Frisian. In the northeast, Low-Saxon is widely spoken. Both languages have a long history in these regions. The government has taken steps to preserve these languages.

Traders and Wars

In its early days, the Netherlands was part of the Low Countries. This region also included present-day Belgium and Luxembourg. Romans conquered the Low Countries about two thousand years ago. Later, Germanic people, called the Franks, took over.

Little by little, towns grew up along the coast. People lived by

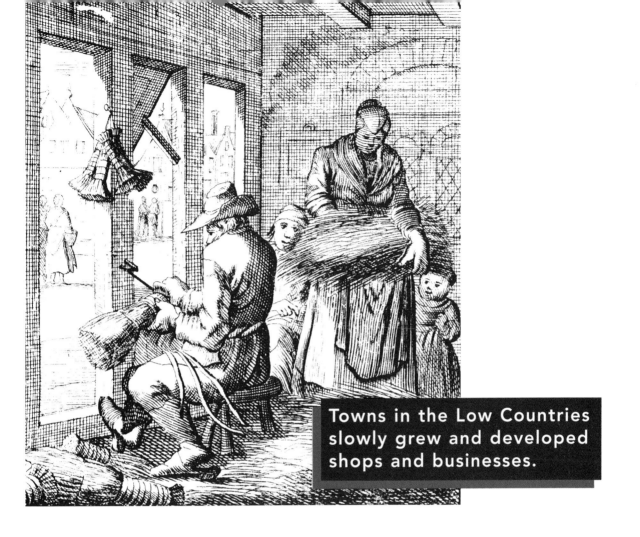

Towns in the Low Countries slowly grew and developed shops and businesses.

fishing and building ships. By the 1200s, the Low Countries had busy cloth and shipbuilding industries. Traders sent their goods by ship to faraway ports.

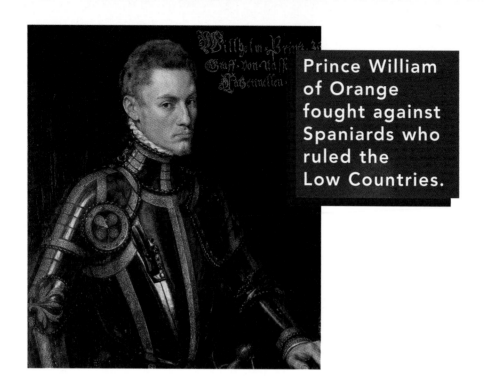

Prince William of Orange fought against Spaniards who ruled the Low Countries.

In the early 1500s, Spain took over the Low Countries. Prince William of Orange led a revolt against Spain in the 1570s. In 1581, the Low Countries' northern provinces declared their freedom. In 1648, Spain yielded to that declaration. This region was now the Dutch Republic, or the Netherlands. The southern provinces later became Belgium.

The 1600s were the Netherlands's Golden Age. Dutch traders became wealthy. They lived in fine homes along the

Many Dutch were wealthy and lived in fancy houses during the Golden Age.

canals. Dutch companies traded with cities all over Europe. Amsterdam became a powerful banking center.

The Dutch fought sea battles with England in the late 1600s. They made peace but soon began fighting with France. Most of these battles were about who would control the valuable sea trade. In 1795, France took control of the Netherlands.

The Golden Age and the Colonies

In 1602, Dutch traders formed the Dutch East India Company. Their ships explored new lands to set up trading colonies. Dutch colonies grew up in Indonesia,

Traders from the Dutch East India Company sailed to new lands to set up trading colonies.

Africa, and Ceylon (present-day Sri Lanka). The traders brought back tea, cocoa, pepper, pearls, exotic birds, and other expensive goods. The wealth from these trading colonies helped to create the Netherlands's Golden Age.

The Dutch West India Company began in 1621. Its ships sailed to North America. There, Dutch settlers founded New Netherlands. Most of this colony became New York State. Its capital, New Amsterdam, is now New York City.

Becoming a Modern Nation

In 1814, the Netherlands was free once again. William, another prince of Orange, was crowned King William I. He ruled the new Kingdom of the Netherlands. At first, Belgium and Luxembourg were part of this kingdom. Later they became separate countries.

William I became king of the Netherlands in 1814.

The Netherlands did not take part in World War I (1914–1918). However, it could not avoid World War II (1939–1945). German forces invaded the Netherlands in 1940. They bombed factories, railroads,

German troops destroyed Rotterdam (above) during World War II. Anne Frank (left) and her family hid from the Germans in Amsterdam.

and bridges. The port city of Rotterdam was destroyed. Food supplies ran low, and many people were starving.

More than 100,000 Dutch Jews died in German camps. The Franks, a Jewish family, hid in an Amsterdam building for two years. Their daughter Anne told her story in *The Diary of Anne Frank*.

The Netherlands's economy recovered quickly after the war. New factories made steel, chemicals, and electronic equipment. In 1992, the Netherlands joined the European Union (EU). Members of the EU help one another develop and grow.

Today, the Kingdom of the Netherlands is a modern, successful country. The Netherlands Antilles and the island of Aruba also belong to the kingdom. These islands were once Dutch colonies, governed by the Netherlands. Now they have their own governments.

Dutch kings and queens still trace their **ancestors** back to the rulers of Orange. However, they do not have much power. The prime minister is the head

The Netherlands Antilles (right) and Aruba (below)

of government. The national lawmaking body is the States-General. Its members are elected by the people.

From Windmills to World Exports

Windmills are a common sight in the Netherlands. The Dutch first used windmills to pump water from their lowlands. Farmers used windmills to grind grain. Windmills also powered the Netherlands's early factories.

Windmills (left) have been very important throughout the Netherlands's history. Delft pottery (below) is an example of the fine crafts made in the Netherlands.

Today, Dutch factories make metals, chemicals, electronics equipment, and airplanes. Craftspeople in Delft make blue-and-white pottery, and

Amsterdam is a diamond-trading center. The Netherlands also has a rich supply of natural gas. However, foods are the Netherlands's most valuable products.

Farmland covers more than half the country. Much of this land is grassy meadows where cows graze. Cow's milk is made into butter, cheese, and other dairy products. The Netherlands is the world's largest **exporter** of cheese. Gouda and Edam are

Cheese is one of the many products that the Dutch make from cow's milk (left). Cows graze in a country meadow (below).

the best-known Dutch cheeses. They are named for the cities that first produced them hundreds of years ago. Many cities still hold weekly cheese markets.

The Netherlands grows more tulips than any other country.

The Netherlands is also famous for its tulips. In the 1600s, the Dutch developed many different types of tulips. They were expensive, and only wealthy people could buy them. Today the Netherlands is the world's largest producer of tulips.

Dutch farmers also grow wheat, barley, fruits, potatoes, and sugar beets. They grow vegetables and flowers in huge greenhouses, as well as outdoors.

In 1815, a Dutch inventor named Johannes Van Houten made cocoa, or powdered chocolate. He also found a way to take the bitter taste out of chocolate. Now Dutch cocoa is served as hot chocolate. The Dutch also make delicious chocolate candy.

Daily Life and Special Traditions

The Dutch people are very careful in using their land. They do not take up valuable space with yards. Instead, most city people live in apartment buildings or **row houses**. In farming regions, fields begin right outside the farmhouse.

Almost everyone in the Netherlands has a bicycle. Riding a

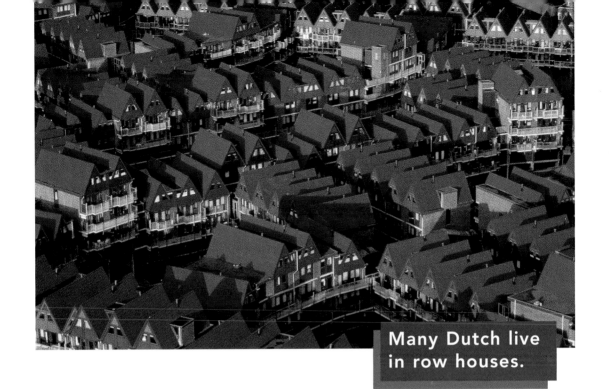

Many Dutch live in row houses.

bike is often the easiest way to travel or shop. Even a bank president may ride a bike to work.

Dutch people eat lots of cheese. A hearty dinner always includes potatoes, too. Another popular food is raw herring (a fish) with onions on top.

Favorite sweets are cookies, pudding, and *drop*. Drop is a salty-sweet **licorice** candy.

Most Dutch people dress as other Europeans do. In some small towns, however, people dress in the **traditional** Dutch folk costume. They wear wooden shoes called *klompen*. Men wear

These colorful wooden shoes are called klompen.

wide, baggy pants. Women wear crisp, white bonnets. Their dresses have colorful flower designs and big skirts.

December 5 is the eve of the feast of Sinterklaas, or Saint Nicholas. This kindly old man brings gifts for children that

Saint Nicholas greets children during the feast of Sinterklaas.

night. Grown-ups write a funny poem with each gift they give. Dutch settlers brought the Sinterklaas feast to North America. Sinterklaas's name became Santa Claus.

In December, families put up Christmas trees, wreaths, and candles. On Christmas Day, they sing carols and eat Christmas *stollen*. This round bread is filled with almond paste and sweet fruits. On New Year's Eve, church bells ring and fireworks explode. People fill the streets

Crowds watch the colorful fireworks on New Year's Eve (above). The country celebrates Queen Beatrix's (right) birthday on April 30.

to wish their neighbors a happy new year.

April 30 is Queen's Day. It honors the birthday of Queen Beatrix. Everyone turns out for parades, street markets, and fairs.

Children around the world enjoy the story of Hans Brinker. In the Netherlands, Hans is a hero. Legend says that he discovered a hole in a dike. Seawater was pouring in and Hans saved the country by putting his finger into the hole. He is the perfect hero for this land by the sea!

Organizations and Online Sites

The Holland Ring
http://www.thehollandring.com

For information on Dutch culture, customs, holidays, folklore, and history

Netherlands Board of Tourism
355 Lexington Avenue, 19th floor
New York, NY 10017

Royal Netherlands Embassy
http://www.netherlands embassy.org/f_explorer.html

For information about The Netherlands and its government, history, and culture

Welcome to Holland
http://www.visitholland.com/

To learn about interesting cities, sights, and customs in The Netherlands

Important Words

ancestors a person's relatives who lived long ago

canals narrow waterways made by humans

dike a high wall to hold water back

exports goods that a country sells to other countries

landscapes wide views of the outdoors

licorice candy flavored with the root of an herb

minority a small number or group within a larger group

province a section within a country

row houses houses connected together in a long line

traditions the customs and beliefs of a group of people

Index

Meet the Author

Ann Heinrichs grew up in Arkansas and lives in Chicago, Illinois. She has written more than eighty books about American, European, Asian, and African history and culture. Several of her books have won national and regional awards.

Besides the United States, she has traveled in Europe, North Africa, the Middle East, and east Asia. The desert is her favorite terrain.

Ms. Heinrichs holds bachelor's and master's degrees in piano performance. She practices t'ai chi empty-hand and sword forms and has won many awards in martial arts competitions.